COUNTRIES IN OUR WORLD

GERMANY
IN OUR WORLD

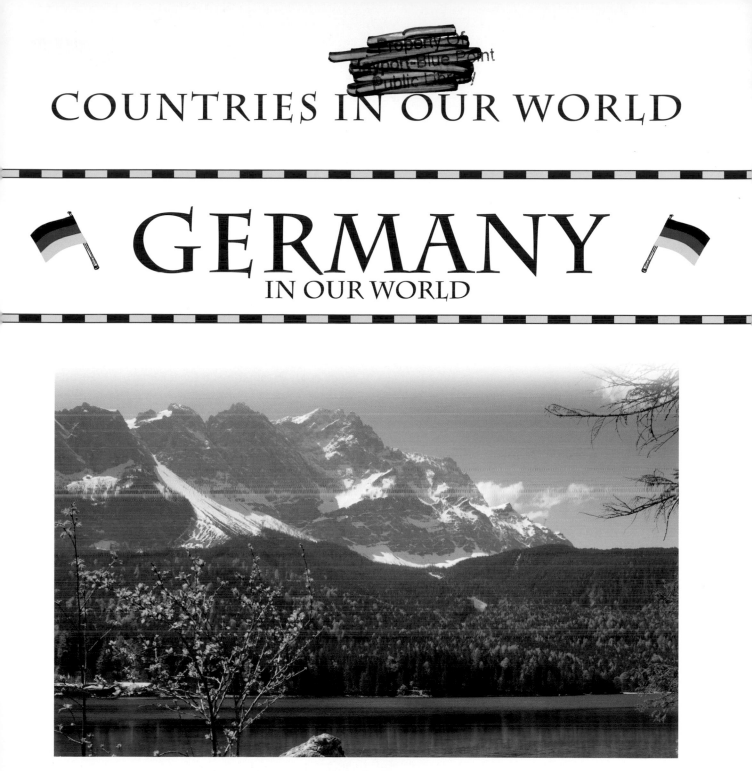

Michael Burgan

A⁺
Smart Apple Media

Published by Smart Apple Media
P.O. Box 3263, Mankato, Minnesota 56002

U.S. publication copyright © 2012 Smart Apple Media.
International copyright reserved in all countries. No
part of this book may be reproduced in any form
without written permission from the publisher.

Printed in the United States of America at Corporate
Graphics, in North Mankato, Minnesota.

Published by arrangement with the Watts Publishing
Group LTD, London.

Library of Congress Cataloging-in-Publication Data

Burgan, Michael.
  Germany in our world / by Michael Burgan.
      p. cm. -- (Countries in our world)
  Includes bibliographical references and index.
  Summary: "Describes the geography, landscape,
economy, government, and culture of Germany today
and discusses Germany's influence of and relations
with the rest of the world"--Provided by publisher.
  ISBN 978-1-59920-387-4 (library binding)
  1. Germany--Juvenile literature. I. Title.
  DD17.B87 2011
  943--dc22

                              2010031669

1305
3-2011

9 8 7 6 5 4 3 2 1

Produced by White-Thompson Publishing, Ltd.
Series consultant: Rob Bowden
Editor: Sonya Newland
Designer: Clare Nicholas
Picture researcher: Amy Sparks

Contents

Introducing Germany

Germany is one of the most powerful nations in Europe with the largest economy and the second-largest population. The Germans are famous for their hard work and skill with advanced technology. The country's great wealth makes it a world leader in economic and political affairs.

Where in the World?

Germany lies in the center of Europe. It is bordered to the east by Poland and the Czech Republic. To the south are Austria and Switzerland. On Germany's western border lie France, Luxembourg, Belgium, and the Netherlands. To the north is Denmark, as well as the North and Baltic seas.

A Troubled Past

For centuries, the area that is now Germany was made up of separate states ruled by dukes and princes. By 1871, many of these small German-speaking countries had united to form the German Empire. After losing World War I (1914–18), life was difficult for the German people. In 1939, the German leader Adolf Hitler tried to expand the country's borders by invading other countries. This sparked World War II (1939–45) and led to the Holocaust—the killing of six million European Jews. Hitler had also ordered the murders of five million other innocent people including gypsies, Catholics, and people with disabilities. Today, people around the world still try to understand how this event happened. They also try to make sure nothing like it ever happens again.

▲ *Germany's position in the heart of Europe has helped it become a powerful leader in areas such as trade and politics.*

4

Building a New Germany

After losing the war, Germany was divided into two nations, West Germany and East Germany. West Germany became one of the world's strongest economies. The communist Soviet Union gained control over East Germany resulting in their limited freedom. In 1989, the Soviet Union gave up its control, and the two German nations soon reunited as a free country. Since then, Germans have worked to overcome problems of the past. The west still has many more people and a stronger economy, but all Germans are proud of their country and work to make it better.

BASIC DATA
Official name: **The Federal Republic of Germany**
Capital: **Berlin**
Size: **134,847 sq miles (357,022 sq km)**
Population: **82,282,988 (2010 est.)**
Currency: **Euro**

▼ *The Brandenburg Gate in the capital, Berlin, was built in the 1800s as a symbol of peace.*

World Connections

Today, Germany is the wealthiest member of the European Union (EU), an association of 27 countries that work together on issues of trade, security, and human rights. Germany is a world leader in international trade and is also generous in aiding other nations. In 2009, it spent almost US$8 billion on foreign aid and plans to give more in the future.

Language and People

Within Europe, Germany has a language link to several German-speaking lands around it including Austria, Liechtenstein, and Switzerland, where German is commonly spoken. Small groups of German-speakers also live in countries such as Belgium and Poland, and even in Germany's former colonies in Africa, including Namibia and Rwanda. Over the centuries, Germans have also migrated to the United States, Canada, and Brazil. The culture they brought—their language, food, religion, and music—helped shape the growth of their adopted homelands.

▶ *The German influence can be seen in the architecture of many of its former African colonies. This German-style church is in Windhoek, Namibia.*

▲ *Literacy rates are high in Germany. About 99 percent of the population can read and write.*

Looking Ahead

Germany recovered more quickly than other European nations from the global recession that began in 2008. Its strong economy means Germany will continue to play an important role in international affairs. At home, the biggest challenge the country faces is a shrinking population. This means that German companies may need to find workers from overseas. However, developing technology may help the country find ways of doing business with fewer workers, which could help keep Germany strong.

IT STARTED HERE

Printing

Books were rare in Europe until a German named Johannes Gutenberg created a new printing process. The Chinese had already printed books, but during the 1450s, Gutenberg developed metal type and a press to print the type on to paper. These improvements made book printing much easier. Today, Germany publishes about 95,000 book titles each year, one of the highest rates in the world.

Landscapes and Environment

With mountains to the south, two of the world's largest seas to the north, and forests and fields in between, Germany has a variety of landscapes. Some of the world's most famous rivers also wind across the country.

Highs and Lows

The Alps mountain range runs through a small part of southern Germany and is the home of Zugspitze, the country's highest peak at 9,721 feet (2,963 m). Smaller mountains and hills surround the area and the central part of Germany also has uplands that can rise to more than 3,280 feet (1,000 m). North Germany is much lower with some stretches sitting below sea level. Germany has several islands in the north situated in the Baltic and North seas.

▼ *Zugspitze stands on Germany's border with Austria. Snow covers the mountain for more than half the year making it popular with skiers and snowboarders.*

Forests

Around 30 percent of Germany's land area is covered in forest including the Black Forest in Baden-Wurttemberg. Over the centuries, people have cleared spruce, fir, and pine trees, and in more recent years, pollution has killed large parts of the forest. Still, many trees remain and wood from some of them is used to make clocks that are famous around the world. Further east, the Bavarian Forest stretches into the Czech Republic forming part of the largest continuous forest in Europe. Thuringia, in central Germany, has beech, spruce, and pine forests that are well-known for their beauty.

▲ *Germany's forests are popular destinations for both German and foreign tourists who enjoy hiking through the beautiful landscape.*

PLACE IN THE WORLD
Total area: 134,847 sq miles (357,022 sq km)
Percentage of world land area: 0.24%
World ranking: 62nd

Waterways and Lakes

The Rhine River—the longest river in Germany—actually begins in the Swiss Alps and also flows through France and the Netherlands before reaching the North Sea. The part of the Rhine that runs through Germany is the busiest waterway in Europe, as boats carrying both people and goods sail on it. Another river, the Elbe, was once part of the boundary between East and West Germany. Other important rivers include the Moselle, the Main, the Oder, and the Ruhr. The country shares its largest lake, Lake Constance (Bodensee), with neighboring Austria and Switzerland.

IT'S A FACT!

Starting as a spring in southwest Germany, the Danube eventually becomes Europe's second-longest river, flowing for 1,725 miles (2,776 km). The river and the canals connected to it help link Germany with many neighboring nations forming a waterway that runs from the North Sea to the Black Sea.

▼ *The Rhine Valley is dotted with medieval castles, towns, and villages. It is now prestigiously listed as a World Heritage Site.*

Wildlife

Germany is home to a variety of wildlife. Wild boars and deer roam through some forests, and many kinds of water birds live along the country's lakes and rivers. Germany also has several endangered species including the wildcat. Once found in many German states, only a few thousand of these cats exist today. The Germans have built bridges over some roads just for animals to use, hoping to keep cars from killing them.

Climate

The majority of Germany has a temperate climate. In most places, the temperature does not drop sharply in winter or soar in summer. Areas closest to the North and Black seas tend to have warmer winters and cooler summers than the rest of the country. It can rain at any time, but rainfall tends to be higher during the summer. The areas around the Alps sometimes experience a warm wind off the mountains called a *foehn*.

▲ *Red deer roam throughout Germany's forests even in the coldest winter months.*

GOING GLOBAL

Millions of years ago, many different animals made their homes around a lake near Darmstadt in southwest Germany. The lake is now gone, but fossils of the creatures remain. In the Messel Pit, people have found bones from prehistoric crocodiles, mammals, insects, and fish. The pit is the world's best source for fossils from the Eocene period, which began about 57 million years ago. The Messel Pit is now a World Heritage Site.

Population and Migration

With more than 80 million people, Germany has the largest population in Europe apart from Russia. Despite the arrival of many immigrants, the German population is declining and it could soon be overtaken by other European countries.

The German People

The majority of Germans have roots in their homeland, and most live in the former West Germany, which was about twice as large as East Germany. One notable ethnic group is the Turks, who make up 2.4 percent of the population. Other immigrants have come from Italy, Spain, Greece, Poland, and Russia. Almost 75 percent of the people live in cities or nearby urban areas. Berlin, the capital, is the largest city with a population of 3.4 million. Other big cities include Hamburg, Munich, Cologne, and Frankfurt. Several others have populations of more than 500,000.

▶ *Munich is the third largest city in Germany with a population of around 1.3 million.*

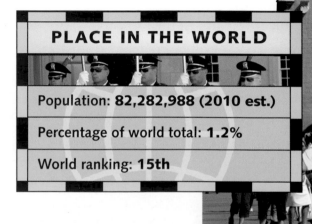

PLACE IN THE WORLD

Population: **82,282,988 (2010 est.)**

Percentage of world total: **1.2%**

World ranking: **15th**

East and West

Since reunification, almost two million of the 16 million former East Germans have moved west. Most of them are well-educated young women seeking jobs in large cities. The people who remain in the east are mostly the elderly or young men without skills.

Some eastern cities have lost up to 30 percent of their population since 1990. Some visitors to the east describe seeing empty homes left by people who headed west. A much smaller number of Germans from both the east and west leave the country each year to look for work in other countries. Most head to other German-speaking countries such as Switzerland and Austria, but some settle farther away in countries such as the United States, which has attracted German immigrants for centuries.

IT'S A FACT!

Germany has five distinct minority groups. The Danes live mostly in Schleswig-Holstein, which once belonged to Denmark. The Friesians live near the Netherlands and the North Sea. The Sinti and Roma, traditionally nomadic, are spread throughout the country. The Sorbs live in eastern Germany. Each group has its own language, which the German government encourages them to use.

◀ *German-Americans march in a parade on Steuben Day in New York.*

A Falling Population

More and more people in Germany are deciding not to have children or to have fewer children than in previous generations. This has led to a population decline across the country. Today, Germany has one of the lowest birth rates in the world. In 2007, the government began offering couples money so they could take more time off work to raise children. Still, the birth rate did not rise enough to stop the falling population.

Immigration

During the 1950s and 1960s, West Germany welcomed immigrants from Turkey, Italy, and other European nations. The newcomers were called *Gastarbeiters*, or "guest workers." Most took low-paying jobs that the Germans did not want. Many *Gastarbeiters* made Germany their permanent home and raised families there. East Germany saw several waves of immigrants from Vietnam. Some originally came to study and stayed to begin careers, while others signed contracts to work there.

▶ *Despite efforts to encourage people to have more children, the birth rate in Germany is still slowing down. A falling birth rate means hospitals such as this one have plenty of room for newborn babies.*

IT'S A FACT!

The German birth rate has declined steadily since the 1950s and is now the lowest in Europe, a position it shares with Italy. The birth rate is 8.21 births per 1,000 population. By comparison, the birth rate in France is 12.43, the UK is 10.67, and Spain is 9.54.

Immigrants Today

Since reunification, the number of immigrants to Germany has fallen from more than one million per year to less than 700,000 in 2007. A lack of jobs has stopped the flow into the country, especially in the east. The Vietnamese are the largest immigrant group in Germany, and many run their own restaurants or other businesses. Most new immigrants choose to settle in the west. In the cities of Stuttgart and Frankfurt, about 40 percent of the population are foreign-born or the descendants of recent immigrants. In the east, Berlin has a large ethnic population. About 25 percent of the residents have foreign roots.

▼ *Turkish shops and restaurants cater to the large Turkish population in Germany.*

GOING GLOBAL

Immigration from Turkey has given Germany a Turkish flair. Some 800,000 Turks have taken German citizenship. Even though younger Turks are becoming more comfortable speaking German, the government is encouraging them to continue to learn and speak Turkish, the country's second-most used language.

Culture and Lifestyles

Fueled by one of the finest education systems in the world, Germany has been the birthplace of many great thinkers, artists, and writers. Germans have also made technology a large part of their lives—the country has more Internet users than any other European nation.

A Variety of Religions

The Roman Catholic Church is one of several major Christian faiths in Germany, claiming more than 26 million members. In 2005, Joseph Ratzinger became the first German pope in almost 500 years when he was ordained Pope Benedict XVI. The Evangelical Church, a union of several smaller faiths, is the major Protestant religion. Germany's Jews once played a major role in the country's cultural life, but the rise of Hitler forced many to flee, and most of the others were killed. Fewer than 200,000 Jews live in Germany today. Muslims are a growing religious group, numbering close to four million.

▶ *German Pope Benedict XVI is the leader of the Roman Catholic Church. About 34 percent of Germans are Catholics.*

IT STARTED HERE

The Protestant Reformation

In 1517, in the German city of Wittenberg, Martin Luther challenged the authority of the Roman Catholic Church by starting the Protestant Reformation. Catholics across Germany and other parts of Europe began to form new Christian religions that stressed the importance of following the Bible, not rules created by religious leaders. Luther's ideas led to the creation of Lutheranism, a Protestant faith that is now practiced in dozens of countries.

A Land of Ideas

Over the past few centuries, German philosophers such as Immanuel Kant and Friedrich Nietzsche have influenced people around the world. Karl Marx and Friedrich Engels helped create communism, a government system used today in several nations, including China. German scientists have also played major roles in world history. Wernher von Braun developed powerful rockets, while Max Planck helped create modern physics.

Great Writers

Germany's best writers, including Herman Hesse, Günther Grass, and Thomas Mann, are world famous, and their books have been translated into many languages. During the nineteenth century, brothers Jacob and Wilhelm Grimm collected and published German folktales. Such stories as *Snow White* and *Sleeping Beauty* are now read in more than 100 languages around the world.

FAMOUS GERMAN

Johann Wolfgang Goethe (1749–1832)

Perhaps Germany's greatest thinker, Goethe was a scientist and philosopher, as well as a poet and writer. His most famous work, *Faust*, tells the story of a man who gives his soul to the devil. In return, the devil promises to help Faust get whatever he wants. *Faust*, a play, has been performed all over the world and has inspired other artistic works.

▶ *This statue of Goethe stands in Leipzig where he spent three years studying law.*

▲ *The Berlin Philharmonic Orchestra was formed over 100 years ago and is now considered one of the best orchestras in the world.*

Masters of Music

Some of the world's greatest composers were German. Starting at the end of the eighteenth century, Ludwig von Beethoven wrote nine symphonies, as well as other pieces that are still performed all over the world. In the nineteenth century, Richard Wagner wrote a series of operas called *The Ring*, which are among the best-known operas of all time. In modern popular music, the band Kraftwerk has greatly influenced other artists with its use of electronic keyboards and drums since the 1970's.

FAMOUS GERMAN

Johann Sebastian Bach (1685–1750)

Born to a musical family in Thuringia, Bach was a church organist and composer. He wrote many pieces for keyboards, as well as works for both large and small musical groups. His most famous pieces include the *Brandenburg Concertos* and the *Goldberg Variations*. Modern musicians still perform Bach's music and sometimes borrow his melodies for their own works.

The Visual Arts

Germany has had many fine artists whose works are displayed around the world. One of the first was Albrecht Dürer, who was known for his engravings of scenes from the Bible and everyday life. In more recent times, Germans have had a big influence on the development of movies. In 1922, F. W. Murnau made the first vampire movie, *Nosferatu*. He later went to work in the United States, and his influence there helped develop the modern film industry.

Sports

Germans love sports of all kinds. They have excelled in soccer and events at both the Summer and Winter Olympic Games. Since the modern Games began in 1896, only two other nations have won more medals. Germany's Olympic Sports Association helps train more than 27 million athletes, both amateur and professional—more than any other national sports association. Great individual athletes include the skater Katerina Witt, tennis star Steffi Graf, and Formula One racing car champion Michael Schumacher.

IT STARTED HERE

Movies

Two German brothers, Max and Emil Skladanowsky, were the first people to show movies to a paying audience. They invented a machine called the Bioskop, an early film projector. Their presentation took place in Berlin in 1895 and amazed the people who came to view it.

▼ *Michael Schumacher won the Formula One championship seven times between 1994 and 2004.*

▶ *Lena Schoeneborn of Germany celebrates a gold medal for the pentathlon at the 2008 Beijing Olympics.*

Economy and Trade

Germany makes a variety of goods that are sold around the globe, helping to create the world's fourth-largest economy. More than half of Germany's exports are sold to other European Union nations.

An Advanced Economy

BMW and the Daimler Group are just two German vehicle manufacturers. Together these car companies make Germany the world's fourth-largest car manufacturer. Germany is also a leading maker of electronic goods and communications technology with Siemens as an important company. The service industry makes up the largest part of the nation's economy, by employing more than 28 million people. Service industries include banking, government, transportation, and retail stores. To keep Germany's economy growing, both companies and the government spend billions of euros each year on research.

IT STARTED HERE

Cars

In 1885, German inventor Karl Benz put a gasoline-powered engine on a three-wheeled vehicle and created what is considered to be the world's first automobile. His company later became part of Mercedes Benz, owned by the Daimler Group.

▼ *A worker in a German BMW factory. Other famous German car manufacturers include Volkswagen and Porsche. Their vehicles are sold worldwide.*

Farms and Forests

Farming makes up only a small part of the German economy, yet German farms produce about 80 percent of the country's food. Among European Union nations, Germany is the leading producer of milk and pork. It is also among the leaders in beef, potato, and grain production. Leading food exports include *wursts* (sausages) and cheeses. Germany also produces beer and wine, which are sold both at home and abroad. Germany's many forests provide wood used in a variety of ways. Lumber is used for building, and trees also provide the raw material for paper.

Natural Resources

Germany's most important natural resources are iron, coal, and potash, a chemical used in farming among other things. Germany's iron and coal are used to make steel. The country is one of the largest steel producers in the world, and the largest in Europe. However, the industry suffered during the worldwide economic troubles of 2008–09 along with other German industries.

GLOBAL LEADER

Coal Production

Germany produces more lignite—also called brown or soft coal—than any other nation. This type of coal is commonly used to generate electricity, and 24 percent of Germany's electricity comes from power plants fueled by lignite.

◀ *The Weisweiler power plant uses lignite to generate electricity, but there are concerns about the polluting gases released in the process.*

Beyond Germany's Borders

Germany was a founding member of the European Union and one of the first EU members to replace its own currency with the euro. With the largest economy in the EU, Germany's economic strength is important for the entire region. Although Germany is a leading exporter, it does not sell as many high-tech goods abroad as several other EU nations. The country needs more engineers to produce more goods in high-tech industries, such as information technology and communications.

FAMOUS GERMANS
Karl (b. 1920) and Theo (b. 1922) Albrecht

Theo Albrecht first sold groceries in his mother's small market. As an adult, he and his brother Karl launched their own grocery store, later called Aldi. The Albrechts sold fewer items and offered fewer services than other stores, but their prices were cheap. Over time, Aldi added non-food items and opened more stores across Germany. Today, the company has stores in many European nations, Australia, and the U.S. The Albrechts are among the richest people in the world.

▼ German supermarket chain Aldi has spread throughout the world with more than 1,000 stores in the United States alone.

Global Groups

Germany belongs to several international organizations that address world issues. At the same time, the member nations of these groups also watch out for their own interests. The Group of Eight (G8) holds meetings between the leaders of the world's eight largest industrial nations. Germany hosted the G8 in 2007. The Group of 20 (G20) includes nations that are quickly expanding their economies, such as Brazil, India, and China.

PLACE IN THE WORLD

Value of economy:
US$3,668,000 million

Percentage of world total: **6%**

World ranking: **4th**

Trading Partners

France is the top customer for German goods followed by the United States and the United Kingdom. Eastern Europe and Asia are growing markets for German goods. Eastern Europe buys about 10 percent of Germany's exports, and sales to Asia tripled between 1993 and 2006. More than 3,500 German companies have operations in Asia. For imports, Germany buys more goods from the Netherlands than from any other nation.

▼ *Container ships like this in the port of Hamburg—the third-largest port in Europe—are loaded with goods to be shipped all over the world.*

Government and Politics

The castles that dot Germany show the role royalty once played in ruling the people. Today, the government is democratic at all levels, and voters choose the people they want to represent them.

The Basic Law

The form of Germany's national government is outlined in the Basic Law. This document was written when West Germany was formed in 1949. As part of the reunification process, East Germans agreed to follow the Basic Law. Under it Germany has a federal system, which means that power is shared between the 16 German states and the national government. States make sure that both national and state laws are enforced. Since 2006, they have had greater control over issues such as education. Within the states, towns and cities have their own elected governments.

▲ *The Reichstag (parliament) building in Berlin. The words over the entrance mean "For the German People."*

IT'S A FACT!

Germany's major parties are the Christian Democratic Union, the Christian Social Union, the Social Democratic Party, the Greens, and the Left Party.

Making Laws

Every four years, voters elect representatives to the Bundestag, the German parliament, which creates Germany's national laws. Another body, the Bundesrat, also shapes the country's laws. The state governments elect its members. They also review all proposed bills and must approve certain ones before they become law. The Bundesrat also reviews issues related to Germany's role in the European Union.

The Role of Parties

The Basic Law gives political parties specific roles in the government. The parties choose the people who run for office and organize their campaigns. In the Bundestag, the party with the most members chooses the chancellor, who is the leader of the

national government. The chancellor selects the ministers who will head important government agencies, such as Defense, Health, and Economics.

◀ *The lower house of the German parliament—the Bundestag—in session.*

Germany and the World

West Germany became a member of the North Atlantic Treaty Organization (NATO) in 1955 and both Germanys joined the United Nations (UN) in 1973. As a UN member, Germany promotes peace and human rights around the world. NATO is a military organization. After World War II, many Germans opposed their country's use of troops in foreign lands. However, today more Germans accept their country's role in certain wars. Germany has sent troops on several NATO missions, mosty recently to Afghanistan.

GOING GLOBAL

Each year, various non-profit groups send several thousand young adults around the world to help other nations. This is thanks to the German government's *Weltwaert* ("World-wards") program, which allows young Germans to help with projects such as caring for orphans in Africa or protecting rainforests in South America.

▼ *German troops—part of the NATO forces— in Afghanistan in 2009.*

From Enemies to Friends

Germany has tried to build better relations with nations it had invaded during World War II, such as France, Poland, and Russia. France and Germany now work closely on trade and defense issues. Poland is slowly improving its ties with Germany, thanks partly to increased trade. Russian and German leaders hold an annual meeting to seek stronger ties.

A Special Foreign Relationship

Soon after World War II, the nation of Israel was formed as a homeland for Jews. West Germany sought good ties with Israel to make up for the suffering Hitler caused European Jews. That policy continues, and Germany has paid more than 26 billion euros to Israeli citizens who survived the Holocaust. German leaders have also tried to improve relations between Israel and its Arab neighbors, who have fought several wars since 1948.

▲ *German chanceller Angela Merkel meets with French prime minister Nikolas Sarkozy in 2009. The two countries now have close ties.*

FAMOUS GERMAN

Konrad Adenauer (1876–1967)

Konrad Adenauer was elected West Germany's first chancellor in 1949. For almost 15 years, he helped repair Germany's relations with its former enemies and create a democratic government. Adenauer also helped restore social order, paving the way for Germany's great economic growth.

Germany in 2020

The world economic crisis hit Germany hard as people lost jobs and cut back on spending. However, Germany recovered more quickly than many other nations and is likely to remain one of the world's richest countries in the years ahead even as it faces new problems.

Changes in the Economy

Germany will move even more towards high-tech industries in the next decade. Traditional industries, such as car-making, may lose jobs to companies overseas. This change will bring a shift in population as people move out of the areas that cut jobs and into the ones where new companies are growing. Germany will have lost its place as the world's top exporter to China, though other nations will still seek German goods.

IT'S A FACT!

A 2009 poll conducted in 21 nations asked which countries had the most positive influence in the world. Germany received the highest rating around the world as it had the year before.

▶ *Germany already has a world-renowned high-tech industry, but it is likely to grow in the coming years.*

A Shrinking Population

Germany's population will be smaller in 2020 for a couple of reasons. First, most young couples will continue to have few or no children. A reduced number of children will result in an older population. The government will struggle to pay for the needs of this larger, more elderly population. Second, the population will shrink as more Germans continue to leave the country. Only immigration will help keep the population from shrinking even more. However, immigrants could face tough times as Germany may have trouble providing services, such as healthcare and education, for all the new arrivals.

New Sources of Energy

The world will continue to fight global warming with Germany likely to play a key role. German engineers are already world leaders in technologies that reduce the use of fossil fuels, which worsen global warming. In 2020, about 25 percent of the country's electricity will come from renewable energy sources, such as wind and solar power. Germany will draw on its long tradition of technical skill to help itself and the world in the years ahead.

▼ *A technician puts the finishing touches on the Lieberose Solar Park, which opened in April 2009.*

GLOBAL LEADER

Solar Power

The Lieberose Solar Park in Cottbus, Germany was the world's second-largest solar plant when it was completed in 2009. The park covers an area equal to about 280 football fields and produces enough electricity for 15,000 homes.

Glossary

colonies territories under the immediate political control of a state.

democratic a type of government where people vote for the people they wish to represent them.

economy the financial system of a country or region, including how much money is made from the production and sale of goods and services.

engravings works of art created by digging out part of a material, such as wood or metal to form pictures.

ethnic group a group of people who identify with each other and feel they share a history.

export to transport goods or services to other countries for sale or trade.

federal a system of government with power shared between states and the national government.

fossil fuels fuels formed over millions of years from the remains of ancient life forms.

global warming the gradual rise in temperatures on the surface of the earth caused by changes in the amount of greenhouse gases in the atmosphere.

high-tech relating to electronics or sciences that rely on computers and other devices to produce goods.

immigrants people who have moved to another country to live.

imports brought in goods or services, to a country from other nations.

migrate to move to another country to live or work.

minority a relatively small group of similar people within a large population.

natural resources minerals, plants, or other items from the earth or seas that are used to make products.

philosophers thinkers who study complex issues, such as the meaning of life and death or how people should live together in society.

pollution ruining the environment with man-made waste, such as vehicle emissions, waste gases from factories, or chemicals from fertilizers.

prehistoric dating back before written history.

Reformation a movement that began in Germany where people broke away from Catholicism and established the Protestant Church.

reunification the act of bringing back together two separate countries that were once one.

symphonies long musical pieces for orchestras divided into three or four parts.

World Heritage Site a place that has outstanding universal value and is protected by the UNESCO World Heritage Center.

Further Information

Books

Celebrate Germany
Celebrate!
by Robyn Hardyman
(Chelsea Clubhouse, 2009)

Germany
Country Explorers
by Robin Nelson
(Lerner Publications Company, 2011)

Discover Germany
Discover Countries
by Camilla De la Bedoyere
(PowerKids Press, 2010)

Looking at Germany
Looking at Countries
by Kathleen Pohl
(Gareth Stevens Pub., 2008)

Web Sites

https://www.cia.gov/library/publications/the-world-factbook/geos/gm.html
CIA World Factbook – Germany. From the spy agency of the US government, this site includes a map and current statistics on Germany and its people.

http://europa.eu/europago/welcome.jsp and http://europa.eu/youth
These European Union sites have been set up especially for children and young people.

http://www.tatsachen-ueber-deutschland.de/389.0.html
Sponsored by the German government, this site looks at the country's culture, economy and geography, among other topics, and offers links to other useful sites.

http://www.infoplease.com/ipa/A0107568.html
All the knowledge you need about Germany, including statistics, maps, facts and figures, and history of the country.

Every effort has been made by the publisher to ensure that these web sites contain no inappropriate or offensive material. However, because of the nature of the Internet, it is impossible to guarantee that the content of these sites will not be altered. We strongly advise that Internet access is supervised by a responsible adult.

Index

Numbers in **bold** indicate pictures